"HOMECOMING" JINGLE BE

J.S. Pierpoint
Arranged by DAVE BRUBECK

Moderately fast ♩ = 160

Like sleigh bells

(with pedal)

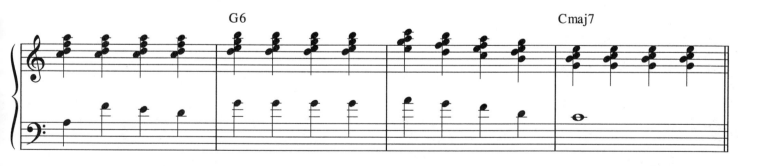

"Homecoming" Jingle Bells - 5 - 1
0157B

4

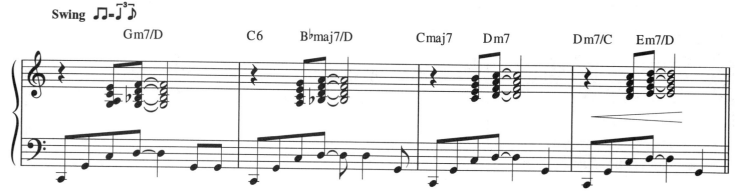

"Homecoming" Jingle Bells - 5 - 2
0157B

elections from
A DAVE BRUBECK
Christmas

Project Manager: Tony Esposito

WARNER BROS. PUBLICATIONS - THE GLOBAL LEADER IN PRINT
USA: 15800 NW 48th Avenue, Miami, FL 33014

WARNER/CHAPPELL MUSIC

CANADA: 15800 N.W. 48th AVENUE
MIAMI, FLORIDA 33014
SCANDINAVIA: P.O. BOX 533, VENDEVAGEN 85 B
S-182 15, DANDERYD, SWEDEN
AUSTRALIA: P.O. BOX 353
3 TALAVERA ROAD, NORTH RYDE N.S.W. 2113
ASIA: UNIT 901 - LIPPO SUN PLAZA
28 CANTON ROAD
TSIM SHA TSUI, KOWLOON, HONG KONG

NUOVA CARISCH

ITALY: VIA CAMPANIA, 12
20098 S. GIULIANO MILANESE (MI)
ZONA INDUSTRIALE SESTO ULTERIANO
SPAIN: MAGALLANES, 25
28015 MADRID
FRANCE: CARISCH MUSICOM,
25, RUE D'HAUTEVILLE, 75010 PARIS

INTERNATIONAL MUSIC PUBLICATIONS LIMITED

ENGLAND: GRIFFIN HOUSE,
161 HAMMERSMITH ROAD, LONDON W6 8BS
GERMANY: MARSTALLSTR. 8, D-80539 MUNCHEN
DENMARK: DANMUSIK, VOGNMAGERGADE 7
DK 1120 KOBENHAVNK

CONTENTS

["

JOY TO THE WORLD

Lowell Mason (1836)
Arranged by DAVE BRUBECK

Joy To The World - 4 - 1
0157B

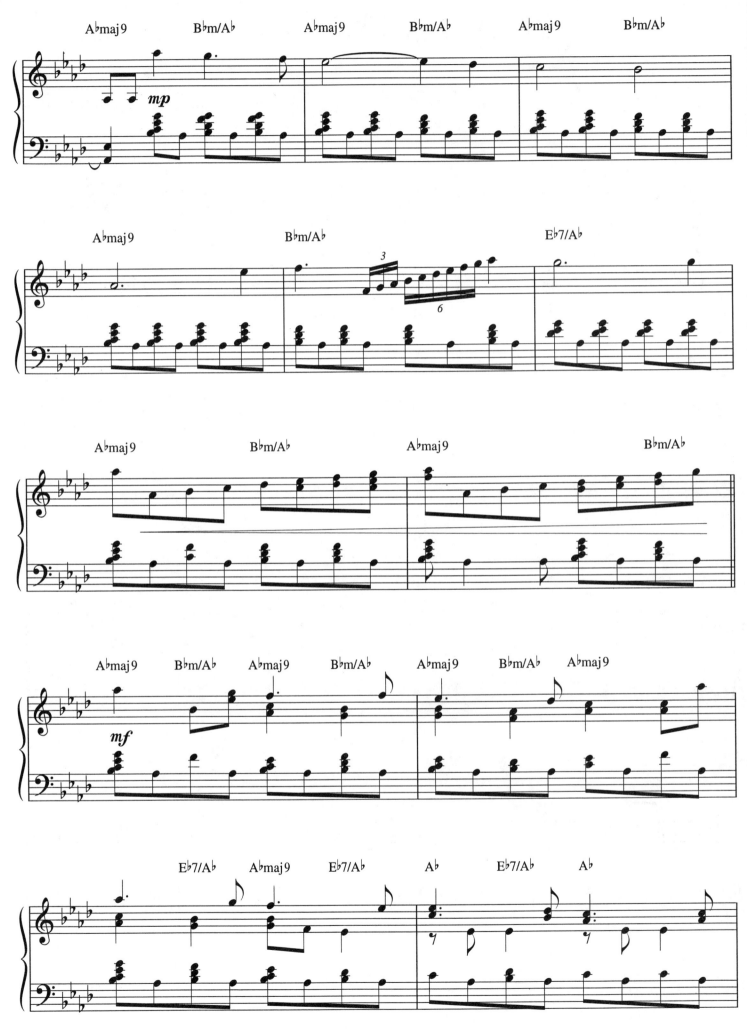

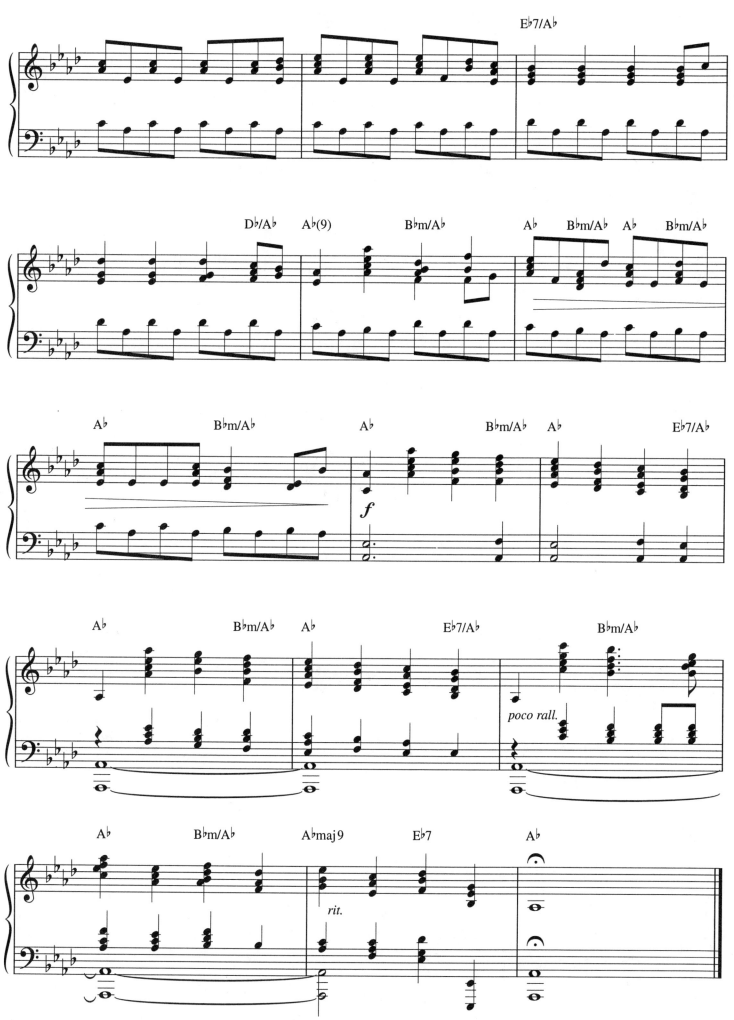

AWAY IN A MANGER

Traditional
Arranged by DAVE BRUBECK

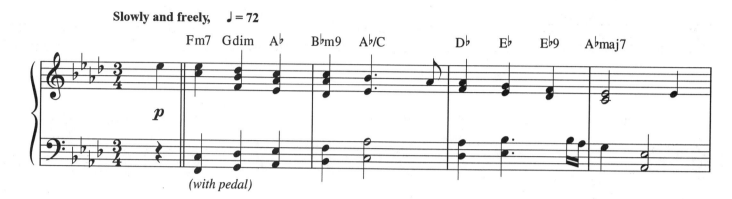

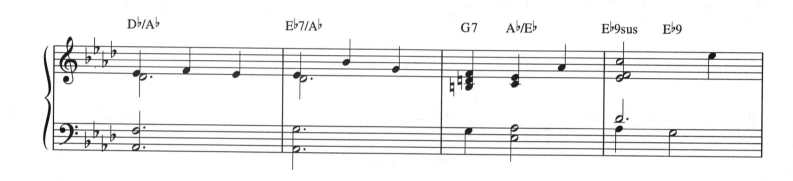

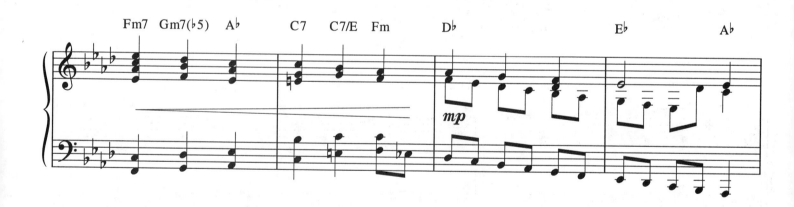

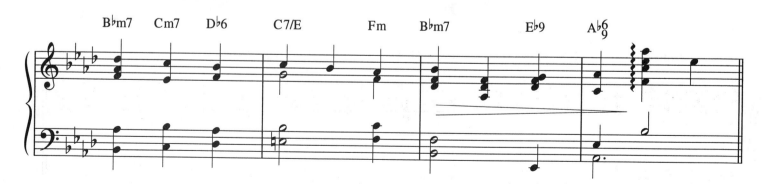

Away In A Manger - 3 - 1
0157B

WINTER WONDERLAND

Music by FELIX BERNARD
Arranged by DAVE BRUBECK

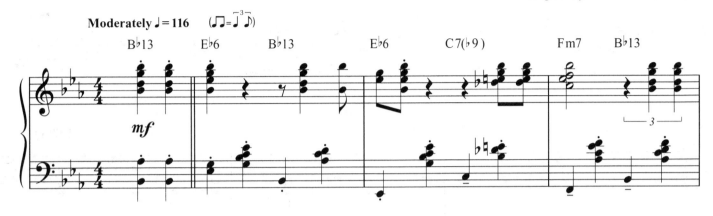

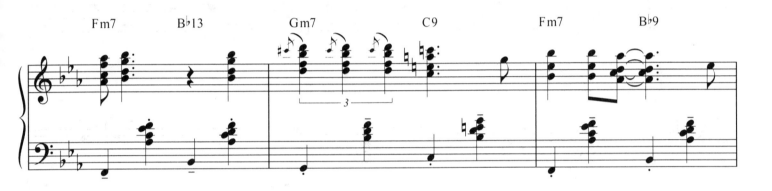

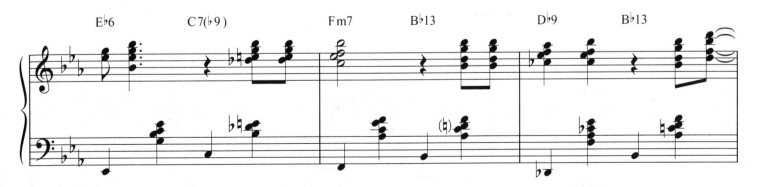

Winter Wonderland - 5 - 1
0157B

WHAT CHILD IS THIS?
(Greensleeves)

Traditional
Arranged by DAVE BRUBECK

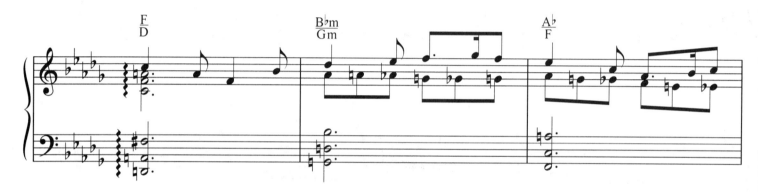

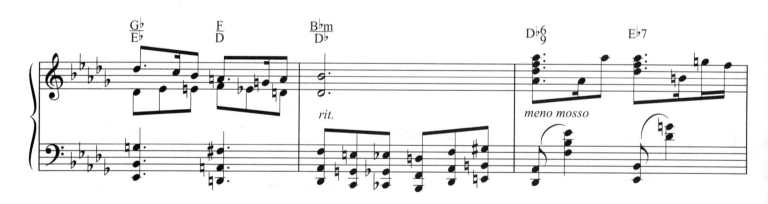

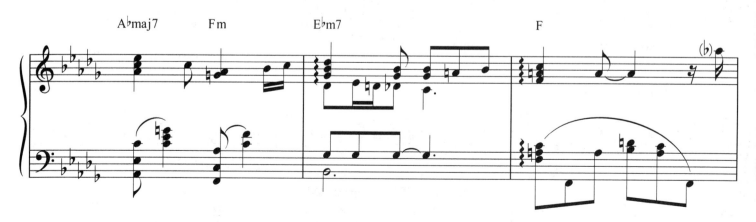

What Child Is This? - 3 - 1
0157B

What Child Is This? - 3 - 2
0157B

TO US IS GIVEN
(From the "PANGE LINGUA Variations")

Arranged by DAVE BRUBECK

24

To Us Is Given - 4 - 2
0157B

For opt. inversion see measure 1

O TANNENBAUM

Traditional German Carol
Arranged by DAVE BRUBECK

O Tannenbaum - 3 - 1
0157B

SILENT NIGHT

Franz Gruber
Arranged by DAVE BRUBECK

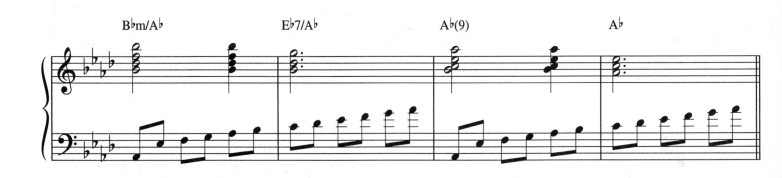

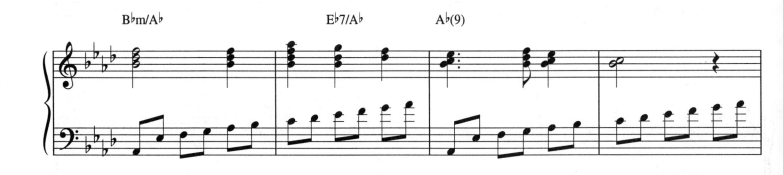

Silent Night - 4 - 4
0157B

CANTOS PARA PEDIR LAS POSADAS

Traditional Mexican Folk Song
Arranged by DAVE BRUBECK